Gift of:
Charlie De Fed

www.mascotbooks.com

The ABCs of Boys' Lacrosse

For more information, please contact:
Mascot Books
560 Herndon Parkway #120
Herndon, VA 20170
info@mascotbooks.com

Library of Congress Control Number: 2016907175

CPSIA Code: PRT0716A
ISBN: 978-1-63177-802-5

Printed in the United States

THIS BOOK IS DEDICATED TO MY NEPHEWS, LEO BENJAMIN AND BRODY RHYS, AS WELL AS ALL OF MY CURRENT AND FORMER COACHES AND TEAMMATES.

The ABCs of Boys' Lacrosse

BY MAX SEIBALD &
JOANNA COOK KJELLMAN

ILLUSTRATED BY CLAIRE LORDON

 IS FOR **ATTACKMEN!** THEY LEAD THE OFFENSE, SCORE GOALS, AND GET **ASSISTS.**

 IS FOR SOLID RUBBER **B**ALL, STICK **B**AG, AND **B**US! THESE ARE JUST SOME OF THE THINGS PLAYERS NEED WHEN THEY TRAVEL TO GAMES.

BOX LACROSSE, ALSO KNOWN AS INDOOR LACROSSE, IS A SIX-ON-SIX GAME PLAYED IN A RINK.

 STANDS FOR **C**OACH. HE LEADS THE TEAM AND TEACHES THE BOYS MORE ABOUT THE GAME.

CLEATS MAKE PLAYING ON GRASS EASY AND FUN!

CRADLE IS THE WAY A PLAYER HOLDS AND MOVES THE BALL IN HIS STICK.

D IS FOR DEFENSEMEN. THEY STOP THE OTHER TEAM FROM SCORING.

DODGE IS A QUICK MOVE TO GET AROUND A DEFENSEMAN.

DADS COME TO WATCH THEIR SONS PLAY.

E REPRESENTS THE **E**NERGY AND **E**XCITEMENT YOU'LL SEE FROM PLAYERS DURING A GAME!

PLAYERS WEAR **E**LBOW PADS ON THEIR ARMS TO PROTECT THEM FROM GETTING HURT.

F STANDS FOR **F**IELD, **F**RIENDS, **F**UN!

FACE-OFF IS THE BATTLE TO GET THE BALL AT THE START OF EACH GAME, EACH PERIOD, AND AFTER EVERY GOAL.

FIELD LACROSSE, ALSO KNOWN AS OUTDOOR LACROSSE, IS A TEN-ON-TEN GAME PLAYED ON TURF OR GRASS.

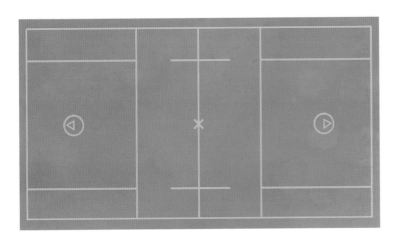

FIL IS THE INTERNATIONAL GOVERNING BODY FOR MEN'S AND WOMEN'S LACROSSE.

 IS FOR **G**OALIE, THE PLAYER WHO TRIES TO STOP THE BALL FROM GOING IN THE GOAL.

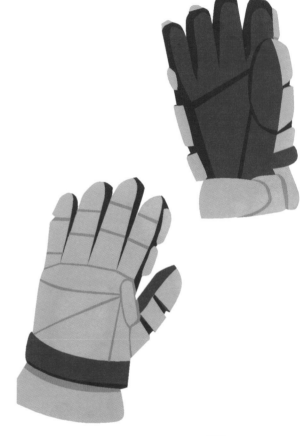

PLAYERS WEAR **G**LOVES TO PROTECT THEIR HANDS.

GROUNDBALL IS WHEN THE BALL IS SCOOPED UP OFF THE GROUND.

STANDS FOR STICK **H**EAD, WHICH YOU USE TO HOLD, CRADLE, SCOOP, AND PASS THE BALL.

YOU WEAR A **H**ELMET TO PROTECT YOUR HEAD.

THE **H**ALFTIME **H**UDDLE IS WHEN THE PLAYERS GET TO TALK AND REST!

IS FOR THE **I**CE PACK YOU USE IF YOU HAVE AN **I**NJURY.

THE **I**ROQUOIS ARE THE **N**ATIVE **A**MERICANS WHO INVENTED MODERN DAY LACROSSE.

J STANDS FOR THE **J**ERSEY YOU WEAR OVER YOUR PADS. IT HAS YOUR NUMBER AND TEAM NAME ON IT.

 **K** IS FOR **K**ICKING. YOU CAN KICK THE BALL WITH YOUR FEET TO A TEAMMATE OR OPEN SPACE SO YOU CAN SCOOP IT UP OFF THE GROUND.

L STANDS FOR **L**ACROSSE AND **L**OVE OF THE GAME! IN BOYS' LACROSSE TWO TEAMS PLAY AGAINST EACH OTHER AND TRY TO SCORE GOALS BY SHOOTING THE BALL INTO THE OTHER TEAM'S NET.

LONG POLE OR **L**ONG STICK IS A SIX-FOOT STICK THAT DEFENDERS USE.

 **IS FOR MOMS** WHO CHEER LOUDLY IN THE STANDS.

MIDDIES ARE THE PLAYERS WHO COVER THE WHOLE FIELD AND PLAY BOTH OFFENSE AND DEFENSE.

 IS FOR **N**CAA, WHICH OVERSEES ATHLETES' ACTIVITIES AT COLLEGES AND UNIVERSITIES.

O

STANDS FOR **O**FFENSE. THEY ARE RESPONSIBLE FOR SCORING GOALS.

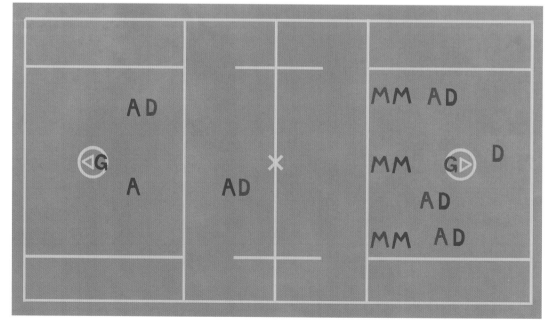

OFF-SIDES IS WHEN TOO MANY PLAYERS ARE ON ONE HALF OF THE FIELD.

P IS FOR **P**RACTICE AND **P**ASSING. **Y**OU CAN PRACTICE WITH FRIENDS OR BY YOURSELF ON A WALL.

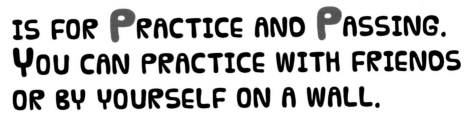

PIPES ARE THE METAL POLES THAT HOLD UP THE NET OF THE GOAL.

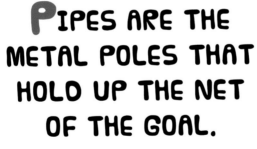

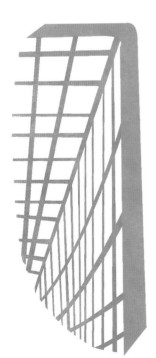

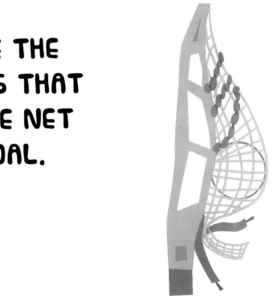

POCKET IS THE STRINGING INSIDE THE HEAD THAT HOLDS THE BALL.

 STANDS FOR **Q**UICKNESS, WHICH IS HOW FAST A PLAYER CAN MOVE.

QUICK STICK, WHERE A PLAYER MAKES A QUICK CATCH AND THROW WITHOUT A CRADLE.

THERE ARE FOUR **Q**UARTERS IN A GAME.

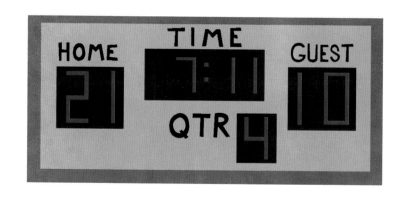

R

IS FOR THE **R**ULES. IT IS IMPORTANT TO KNOW THE RULES OF THE GAME.

RIB PADS THAT YOU WEAR TO PROTECT YOUR RIBS.

S IS FOR THE **S**PORTSMANSHIP TEAMS SHOW AT THE END OF A GAME WHEN THEY SHAKE HANDS.

SHAFT IS THE HANDLE ATTACHED TO THE HEAD TO COMPLETE A STICK.

SHOULDER PADS THAT YOU WEAR TO PROTECT YOUR SHOULDERS.

T

STANDS FOR **T**EAM PHOTO AND **T**ROPHY.

IT'S ALSO FOR THE **T**EWAARATON AWARD, WHICH IS GIVEN TO THE TOP COLLEGE PLAYER EVERY YEAR.

 IS FOR THE **U**SA NATIONAL TEAM AND **U**.S. LACROSSE, THE GOVERNING BODY OF LACROSSE IN THE **U**NITED STATES.

UNIFORM, WHICH ALL THE PLAYERS HAVE TO WEAR.

V REPRESENTS Victory!

 STANDS FOR **W**HISTLE AND **W**ARM-UPS BEFORE GAMES.

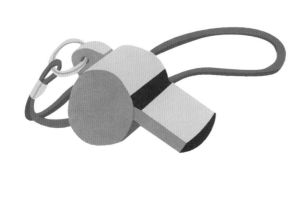

IT ALSO STANDS FOR **W**ALL BALL, ONE OF THE BEST WAYS TO PRACTICE BY YOURSELF.

 IS FOR LA**X**, THE ABBREVIATION FOR LACROSSE.

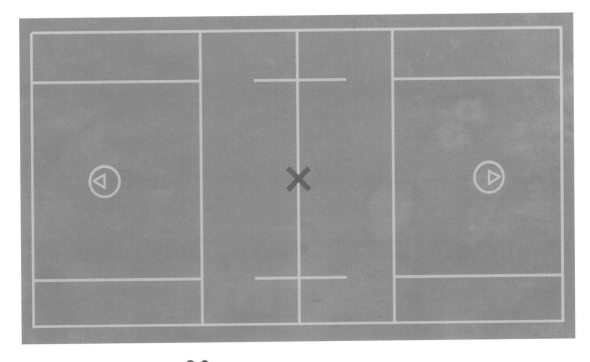

FACE-OFF **X** IS IN THE MIDDLE OF THE FIELD WHERE PLAY IS STARTED.

 STANDS FOR THE **Y**UMMY TREATS
PLAYERS GET TO EAT AFTER A GAME.

THE REFEREE THROWS A **Y**ELLOW FLAG
TO NOTIFY BOTH TEAMS OF A PENALTY.

Z

IS FOR **Z**EBRA, A NICKNAME FOR REFEREES BECAUSE OF THEIR BLACK AND WHITE STRIPES. REFEREES ENFORCE THE RULES OF THE GAME.

About the Authors

MAXWELL SEIBALD IS A HEWLETT HARBOR, NEW YORK, NATIVE WHO LED HIS HIGH SCHOOL TO ITS FIRST EVER COUNTY CHAMPIONSHIP IN 2005. HE WENT ON TO HELP CORNELL UNIVERSITY WIN FOUR CONSECUTIVE IVY LEAGUE CHAMPIONSHIPS, REACH THE FINAL FOUR TWICE, AND THE NCAA CHAMPIONSHIP GAME IN HIS SENIOR YEAR. HE WAS A FOUR-TIME ALL-AMERICAN, THE FIRST PLAYER IN IVY LEAGUE HISTORY TO EARN 1ST TEAM ALL-IVY HONORS FOUR TIMES, AND A TWO-TIME TEAM CAPTAIN. IN 2009, MAX EARNED THE TEWAARATON TROPHY FOR MOST OUTSTANDING COLLEGIATE PLAYER IN THE U.S., THE LT. RAYMOND J. ENNERS AWARD FOR OUTSTANDING PLAYER OF THE YEAR IN DIVISION I, AND THE LT. DONALD MCLAUGHLIN JR. AWARD FOR OUTSTANDING MIDFIELDER OF THE YEAR IN DIVISION I. AS A MEMBER OF THE USA FIELD TEAM IN 2010, MAX WON A GOLD MEDAL AND WAS RECOGNIZED TO THE ALL-WORLD TEAM AS A MIDFIELDER. HE ALSO WON A BRONZE MEDAL AS A MEMBER OF THE USA BOX TEAM IN 2011 AND A SILVER MEDAL WITH THE USA FIELD TEAM IN 2014.

MAX HAS PLAYED PROFESSIONAL LACROSSE IN MAJOR LEAGUE LACROSSE SINCE 2009 AND CURRENTLY PLAYS FOR THE BOSTON CANNONS. HE ALSO PLAYED IN THE NATIONAL LACROSSE LEAGUE FOR THE PHILADELPHIA WINGS FROM 2010-2013. HE HAS BEEN SELECTED AS AN ALL-STAR IN BOTH LEAGUES.

MAX HAS SHARED HIS PASSION FOR PLAYING LACROSSE THROUGH COACHING AND TEACHING AT ALL LEVELS. HE RUNS INSTRUCTIONAL CAMPS, CLINICS, AND CLUB TEAMS ALL OVER THE COUNTRY AND IS AN ACTIVE PARTICIPANT AND BOARD MEMBER OF CITYLAX, A NON-PROFIT ORGANIZATION DEDICATED TO GROWING LACROSSE IN NEW YORK CITY, WHERE HE CURRENTLY RESIDES.

JOANNA COOK KJELLMAN IS A WONDERFUL MOTHER AND GRANDMOTHER WHO IS ALSO A SUCCESSFUL BUSINESSWOMAN. JOANNA WAS ALWAYS A PROUD SUPPORTER AND SUPER FAN OF HER DAUGHTER, KRISTEN KJELLMAN MARSHALL, AND FELL IN LOVE WITH THE SPORT OF LACROSSE THROUGH HER.